To

_____

From

_____

365 DAY
BRIGHTENERS™

for the
Pet Lover's Heart

365 Day Brighteners for the Pet Lover's Heart

Copyright © 2004 DaySpring® Cards, Inc.
Published by Garborg's®, a brand of DaySpring® Cards, Inc.
Siloam Springs, Arkansas
www.dayspring.com

Scripture quotations are from the following sources: The HOLY BIBLE, NEW INTERNATIONAL VERSION® (NIV®) © 1973, 1978, 1984 by International Bible Society. Used by permission of Zondervan Publishing House. The Holy Bible, New Century Version (NCV) © 1987, 1988, 1991 by Word Publishing, Dallas, Texas 75039. Used by permission. THE MESSAGE © Eugene H. Peterson 1993, 1994, 1995. Used by permission of NavPress Publishing Group. All rights reserved. The Living Bible (TLB) © 1971 by permission of Tyndale House Publishers, Inc., Wheaton, IL. The New Revised Standard Version of the Bible (NRSV) © 1989 Division of Christian Education, National Council of Churches. Used by permission of Zondervan Publishing House.

ISBN 1-58061-969-X

Printed in China

365 DAY BRIGHTENERS™

BRIGHTENERS™

for the
Pet Lover's Heart

GARBORG'S®

because every day is a gift

January 1

Did you ever walk into a room and forget why you walked in? I think that is how dogs spend their lives.

SUE MURPHY

January 2

I'm not into working out. My philosophy:
No pain, no pain.

CAROL KOLINSKY

January 3

*G*od must've had a blast. Painting
the stripes on the zebras,
hanging the stars in the sky,
putting the gold in the sunset,
what creativity.

MAX LUCADO

January 4

To bathe a cat takes brute force,
perseverance, courage of conviction—
and a cat. The last ingredient
is usually hardest to come by.

STEPHEN BAKER

January 5

Then God looked over all that he had made,
and it was excellent in every way.

GENESIS 1:31 TLB

January 6

*I*n a cat's eye
all things belong to cats.

ENGLISH PROVERB

January 7

If at first you do succeed—
try to hide your astonishment.

HARRY F. BANKS

January 8

When I play with my cat,
who knows if I am not a pastime
to her more than she is to me.

MICHEL EYQUEM DE MONTAIGNE

January 9

It is a good and safe rule to sojourn
in every place as if you meant to spend your
life there, never omitting an opportunity
of doing a kindness, or speaking
a true word, or making a friend.

JOHN RUSKIN

January 10

The steadfast love of the Lord never ceases,
his mercies never come to an end;
they are new every morning.

LAMENTATIONS 3:22-23 NRSV

January 11

God specializes in things fresh
and firsthand. His plans for you
this year may outshine those of the past....
He's preparing to fill your days
with reasons to give Him praise.

JONI EARECKSON TADA

January 12

Cats are the ultimate narcissists.
You can tell this because of all the time
they spend on personal grooming.
Dogs aren't like this. Dog's idea of personal
grooming is to roll in a dead fish.

JAMES GORMAN

January 13

Beware of people who dislike cats.
They can't be trusted.

January 14

May your troubles in the coming year
be as short-lived as your resolutions.

January 15

If you love someone you will be loyal
to him no matter what the cost.
You will always believe in him,
always expect the best of him, and always
stand your ground in defending him.

1 CORINTHIANS 13:7 TLB

January 16

No animal should ever jump up on
the dining room furniture unless
absolutely certain that he can hold
his own in the conversation.

FRAN LEBOWITZ

January 17

I've learned that you can get by
on charm for about fifteen minutes.
After that, you'd better know something.

January 18

The most common amphibians
are frogs and turtles. A horse would
be called an uncommon amphibian.

A CHILD'S GARDEN OF MISINFORMATION

January 19

We must use time creatively,
and forever realize that the time
is always ripe to do right.

MARTIN LUTHER KING JR.

January 20

The Lord is faithful to all his promises
and loving toward all he has made.

PSALM 145:13 NIV

January 21

Oh, that dog! Ever hear of a German shepherd that bites its nails? Barks with a lisp? You say, "Attack!" And he has one. All he does is piddle. He's nothing but a fur-covered kidney that barks.

PHYLLIS DILLER

January 22

If a person owns a piece of land
do they own it all the way down
to the core of the earth?

January 23

Who was the first person to look at a cow and say, "I think I'll squeeze these dangly things here and drink whatever comes out"?

January 24

Personally, I have always felt the best doctor in the world is the Veterinarian. He can't ask his patients what's the matter. He's just got to know.

WILL ROGERS

January 25

He will give you, through his
great power, everything you need
for living a truly good life:
he even shares his own glory
and his own goodness with us!

2 PETER 1:3 TLB

January 26

Birthdays are good for you.
Statistics show that the people
who have the most live the longest.

LARRY LORENZONI

January 27

One of the advantages of being disorderly is that one is constantly making exciting discoveries.

A. A. MILNE

January 28

Classified Ad: Free Yorkshire Terrier.
8 years old. Hateful little dog.

January 29

God puts each fresh morning,
each new chance of life,
into our hands as a gift to see
what we will do with it.

January 30

*L*et us outdo each other in being
helpful and kind to each other
and in doing good.

HEBREWS 10:24 TLB

January 31

Few delights can equal the mere presence
of one whom we trust utterly.

GEORGE MACDONALD

February 1

If a cat spoke, it would say things like,
"Hey, I don't see the problem here."

ROY BLOUNT JR.

February 2

Nonchalance is the ability
to remain down to earth when
everything else is up in the air.

EARL WILSON

February 3

Things that upset a terrier may pass virtually unnoticed by a Great Dane.

SMILEY BLANTON

February 4

$\mathcal{A}$ good man is concerned
for the welfare of his animals.

PROVERBS 12: 10 TLB

February 5

In my day, we couldn't afford shoes,
so we went barefoot. In the winter we had
to wrap our feet with barbed wire for traction.

BILL FLAVIN

February 6

Don't walk in front of me, I may not follow.
Don't walk behind me, I may not lead.
Walk beside me and just be my friend.

ALBERT CAMUS

February 7

I like pigs.
Dogs look up to us.
Cats look down on us.
Pigs treat us as equals.

WINSTON CHURCHHILL

February 8

$\mathcal{A}$ friend is someone who understands
your past, believes in your future,
and accepts you today just the way you are.

February 9

How precious it is, Lord, to realize
that you are thinking about me constantly!
I can't even count how many times a day
your thoughts turn towards me.

PSALM 139:17-18 TLB

February 10

Faith is what makes life bearable,
with all its tragedies, and ambiguities
and sudden, startling joys.

MADELEINE L'ENGLE

February 11

Cats can be cooperative when something
feels good, which to a cat, is the way
everything is supposed to feel as much
of the time as possible.

ROGER A. CARAS

February 12

No matter how much cats fight,
there always seem to be plenty of kittens.

ABRAHAM LINCOLN

February 13

Friends...lift our spirits, keep us honest,
stick with us when times are tough,
and make mundane tasks enjoyable.
No wonder we want to make friends.

EM GRIFFIN

February 14

See to it that you really do love each
other warmly, with all your hearts.

I PETER 1:22 TLB

February 15

A horse gallops with his lungs,
Perseveres with his heart,
And wins with his character.

TESIO

February 16

Sometimes I lie awake at night and I ask,
"Where have I gone wrong?"
Then a voice says to me, "This is going
to take more than one night."

CHARLES SCHULZ

February 17

*W*holehearted, ready laughter heals,
encourages, relaxes anyone within
hearing distance.

EUGENIA PRICE

February 18

Happiness is like a cat. If you try to coax it or call it, it will avoid you. It will never come. But if you pay no attention to it and go about your business, you'll find it rubbing against your legs and jumping into your lap.

WILLIAM BENNETT

February 19

$\mathcal{I}$ have a dog. His name is Mitzy.
He is black with a long white back.
He licks me in the ear when I come home.
He thinks of me like I think of stamps.

A CHILD'S GARDEN OF MISINFORMATION

February 20

But from everlasting to everlasting
the Lord's love is with those
who fear him, and his righteousness
with their children's children.

PSALM 103:17 NIV

February 21

I like driving around with my two dogs, especially on the freeways. I make them wear little hats so I can use the car-pool lanes.

MONICA PIPER

February 22

*I*n ancient times cats were
worshipped as gods,
they have never forgotten this.

February 23

Dogs feel very strongly that they
should always go with you in the car,
in case the need should arise for them to bark
violently at nothing right in your ear.

DAVE BARRY

February 24

Yet the Lord longs to be gracious to you;
he rises to show you compassion.
For the Lord is a God of justice.
Blessed are all who wait for him!

ISAIAH 30:18 NIV

February 25

Cats are like greatness: Some people are born into cat-loving families, some achieve cats, and some have cats thrust upon them.

WILLIAM H. A. CARR

February 26

A smile costs nothing but gives much.
It takes but a moment, but the memory
of it sometimes lasts forever.

February 27

*L*oneliness isn't such a bad thing,
except when you don't have
anyone to share it with.

BARBARA JOHNSON

February 28

A person who lives in a glass house
should change clothes in the basement.

February 29

Teach us to number our days
and recognize how few they are;
help us to spend them as we should.

PSALM 90:12 TLB

March 1

A dog is like an eternal Peter Pan,
a child who never grows old and who therefore
is always available to love and be loved.

AARON KATCHER

March 2

Blessed are they who have
the gift of making friends,
for it is one of God's best gifts.

THOMAS HUGHES

March 3

To many, the words love, hope,
and dreams are synonymous with horses.

OLIVER WENDELL HOLMES

March 4

$\mathcal{A}$ true friend is one who hears
and understands when you share your deepest
feelings...prods you to personal growth,
stretches you to your full potential.
And most amazing of all, she celebrates
your successes as if they were her own.

RICHARD EXLEY

March 5

$\mathcal{T}$he Lord your God...will take great delight
in you, he will quiet you with his love,
he will rejoice over you with singing.

ZEPHANIAH 3:17 NIV

March 6

Why, then, if not to steal food, would a cat go up on the counter?... Because it is there. Because of the view from the kitchen window. To lick the drips from the tap in the sink. To try to open the cupboards and see what's inside them, maybe to squeeze among the glassware. Or, on a rainy day, to look for small objects to knock off onto the floor and see if they will roll.

BARBARA HOLLAND

March 7

I have a great dog. She's half Lab, half Pit Bull. A good combination. Sure, she might bite off my leg, but she'll bring it back to me.

JIMI CELESTE

March 8

*L*aughing at ourselves as well
as with each other gives
a surprising sense of togetherness.

HAZEL C. LEE

March 9

A bird does not sing because it has an
answer. It sings because it has a song.

CHINESE PROVERB

March 10

Be content with who you are,
and don't put on airs. God's strong hand
is on you; he'll promote you
at the right time. Live carefree
before God; he is most careful with you.

I PETER 5:6-7 THE MESSAGE

March 11

*L*iving in the past is a dull and lonely
business; looking back strains
the neck muscles, causes you to bump
into people not going your way.

EDNA FERBER

March 12

My friend is not perfect—no more than
I am—and so we suit each other admirably.

ALEXANDER SMITH

March 13

There is only one smartest dog in the world, and every boy has it.

March 14

If someone had told me I would be Pope one day, I would have studied harder.

POPE JOHN PAUL I

March 15

The sooner you fall behind,
the more time you'll have to catch up.

*Careful planning puts you ahead in the long run;
hurry and scurry puts you further behind.*

PROVERBS 21:5 THE MESSAGE

March 16

Precious is the parrot who
is trained by a clean tongue.

March 17

Who could believe such pleasure
from a wee ball o' fur?

IRISH SAYING

March 18

A dog can express more
with his tail in minutes than his owner
can express with his tongue in hours.

March 19

Treat your friends as you do your pictures,
and place them in their best light.

JENNIE JEROME CHURCHILL

March 20

This is my prayer: that your love will flourish and that you will not only love much but well. Learn to love appropriately. You need to use your head and test your feelings so that your love is sincere and intelligent, not sentimental gush.

PHILIPPIANS 1:9-10 THE MESSAGE

March 21

You can't keep a good man down—
or an over-affectionate dog.

March 22

Acquiring a dog may be
the only opportunity a human
ever has to choose a relative.

March 23

There are some friends you know you will have for the rest of your life. You're welded together by love, trust, respect or loss— or simple embarrassment.

March 24

She could never be made to comprehend the
great difference between fur and feathers, nor
see why her mistress should gravely reprove her
when she brought in a bird, and
warmly commend when she captured a mouse.

HARRIET BEECHER STOWE

March 25

There is far more to your inner life than
the food you put in your stomach,
more to your outer appearance than
the clothes you hang on your body.
Look at the ravens, free and unfettered,
not tied down to a job description, carefree
in the care of God. And you count far more.

LUKE 12:23-24 THE MESSAGE

March 26

It is in identifying yourself with the hopes, dreams, fears, and longings of others that you may understand them and help them.

WILFERD A. PETERSON

March 27

There's nothing wrong with having nothing to say, as long as you don't say it out loud.

BARBARA JOHNSON

March 28

Say something idiotic and nobody
but a dog politely wags his tail.

VIRGINIA GRAHAM

March 29

Friends find the sweetest sense of happiness
comes from simply being together.

March 30

And God is able to make all grace
abound to you, so that in all things
at all times, having all that you need,
you will abound in every good work.

2 CORINTHIANS 9:8 NIV

March 31

Dogs need to sniff the ground; it's how they keep abreast of current events. The ground is a giant dog newspaper, containing all kinds of late-breaking dog news items, which, if they are especially urgent, are often continued in the next yard.

DAVE BARRY

April 1

Cat's motto: No matter what you've done wrong, always try to make it look like the dog did it.

April 2

Take spring when it comes, and rejoice.
Take happiness when it comes, and rejoice.
Take love when it comes, and rejoice.

CARL EWALD

April 3

I would sooner live in a cottage and wonder at everything than live in a castle and wonder at nothing.

JOAN WINMILL BROWN

April 4

"For I know the plans I have for you," says the Lord. "They are plans for good and not for evil, to give you a future and a hope."

JEREMIAH 29:11 TLB

April 5

Cats are smarter than dogs. You can't get eight cats to pull a sled through snow.

JEFF VALDEZ

April 6

Always remember you're unique,
just like everyone else.

The Lord has made everything for his own purposes.
PROVERBS 16:4 TLB

April 7

The dog is mentioned in the Bible eighteen times—the cat not even once.

W. E. FARBSTEIN

April 8

Jesus' love does not depend upon what we do for Him. Not at all. In the eyes of the King, you have value simply because you are.

MAX LUCADO

April 9

May your unfailing love rest upon us,
O Lord, even as we put our hope in you.

PSALM 33:22 NIV

April 10

Some dogs live for praise—they look at you as if to say "Don't throw balls... just throw bouquets."

JHORDIS ANDERSON

April 11

Don't let people drive you crazy when it is within walking distance.

April 12

*I*t's funny how dogs and cats know the inside of folks better than other folks do.

ELEANOR H. POTTER

April 13

Alexander Hamilton started
the U.S. Treasury with nothing—
and that was the closest our country
has ever been to being even.

WILL ROGERS

April 14

Don't worry about anything; instead,
pray about everything; tell God your needs
and don't forget to thank him for his answers.
If you do this you will experience God's
peace, which is far more wonderful
than the human mind can understand.

PHILIPPIANS 4:6-7 TLB

April 15

Did you ever notice when you put the two words "The" and "IRS" together it spells "THEIRS"?

April 16

The Bible tells us that a sparrow does not fall
without God's notice. I know he will help us
meet our responsibilities through his guidance.

MICHAEL CARDONE SR.

April 17

[One cat to another:]
If you have committed any kind of
an error and anyone scolds you—wash. If you
slip and fall off something and somebody
laughs at you—wash. If somebody calls you
and you don't care to come and still you don't
wish to make it a direct insult—wash.

PAUL GALLICO

April 18

When just being together is more
important than what you do,
you are with a friend.

April 19

*Y*our right hand, O Lord, supports me;
your gentleness has made me great.

PSALM 18:35 TLB

April 20

Cats names are more for human benefit. They give one a certain degree more confidence that the animal belongs to you.

ALAN AYCKBOURN

April 21

Friendship: It involves many things, but, above all, the power of going out of one's self and seeing and appreciating whatever is noble and loving in another.

THOMAS HUGHES

April 22

Silence is golden, and example
is the best teacher, so is a silent example
a golden teacher…or is a silent teacher
a golden example?

April 23

The Pug is living proof that God
has a sense of humor.

MARGOT KAUFMAN

April 24

I have God's more-than-enough,
More joy in one ordinary day....
At day's end I'm ready for sound sleep,
For you, God, have put my life back together.

PSALM 4:6-8 THE MESSAGE

April 25

Quite obviously a cat trusts human beings;
but she doesn't trust another cat because
she knows better than we do.

KAREL CAPEK

April 26

$\mathcal{D}$ear friends, no matter how we find them, are as essential to our lives as breathing in and breathing out.

LOIS WYSE

April 27

Sometimes I make up my mind, other times my mind wanders, and every so often I lose track of it entirely.

April 28

Classified Ad:
Free puppies: $1/2$ Cocker Spaniel,
$1/2$ sneaky neighbor's dog.

April 29

*L*ive out your God-created identity.
Live generously and graciously toward others,
the way God lives toward you.

MATTHEW 5:48 THE MESSAGE

April 30

Dogs give their human companions
unconditional love and are always there
with an encouraging wag of the tail when
they are needed. The dog is indeed
a very special animal.

DOROTHY HINSHAW PATENT

May 1

Riding: The art of keeping a horse between you and the ground.

THE LONDON TIMES

May 2

The child had his mother's eyes, his mother's nose and his mother's mouth. Which left his mother with a pretty blank expression.

ROBERT BENCHLEY

May 3

Hope...is a zany, unpredictable
dependence on a God who loves
to surprise us out of our socks.

MAX LUCADO

May 4

He determines the number of the stars
and calls them each by name.
Great is our lord and mighty in power;
his understanding has no limit.

PSALM 147:4-5 NIV

May 5

Nobody knows if an octopus is waving
its arms or kicking its legs.

A CHILD'S GARDEN OF MISINFORMATION

May 6

Tell someone that there are 400 billion stars and he'll believe you. Tell him a bench has wet paint and he has to touch it.

STEVEN WRIGHT

May 7

For, lo, the winter is past, the rain is over and gone; the flowers appear on the earth; the time of the singing of birds is come.

SONG OF SOLOMON 2:11-12 KJV

May 8

*E*very person's life is a fairy
tale written by God's fingers.

HANS CHRISTIAN ANDERSEN

May 9

Every boy who has a dog should also have a mother, so the dog can be fed regularly.

May 10

When she speaks, her words are wise,
and kindness is the rule
for everything she says.

PROVERBS 31:26 TLB

May 11

The great acts of love are done
by those who are habitually performing
small acts of kindness.

May 12

The good for which we are born into this
world is that we may learn to love.

GEORGE MACDONALD

May 13

The greatest pleasure of a dog is that
you may make a fool of yourself with him
and not only will he not scold you,
but he will make a fool of himself, too.

SAMUEL BUTLER

May 14

There are "friends" who pretend to be friends, but there is a friend who sticks closer than a brother.

PROVERBS 18:24 TLB

May 15

Happiness does not light gently on my shoulder like a butterfly. She pounces on my lap, demanding that I scratch behind her ears.

May 16

To love by freely giving is its own reward.
To be possessed by love and to in turn give love
away is to find the secret of abundant life.

GLORIA GAITHER

May 17

You call to a dog and a dog will
break its neck to get to you.
Dogs just want to please.
Call to a cat and its attitude is,
"What's in it for me?"

LEWIS GRIZZARD

May 18

*F*riendship is precious, not only in the shade,
but in the sunshine of life; and thanks
to a benevolent arrangement of things,
the greater part of life is sunshine.

THOMAS JEFFERSON

May 19

Perfume and incense bring joy to the heart,
and the pleasantness of one's friend
springs from his earnest counsel.

PROVERBS 27:9 NIV

May 20

There is no psychiatrist in the world
like a puppy licking your face.

Ben Williams

May 21

It isn't the big pleasures that count the most;
it's making a great deal out of the little ones.

JEAN WEBSTER

May 22

Sign in an Optometrist's office:
If you don't see what you want,
you've come to the right place.

May 23

Any time you think you have influence,
try ordering around someone else's dog.

May 24

Fix your thoughts on what is true
and good and right. Think about things
that are pure and lovely, and dwell
on the fine, good things in others.

PHILIPPIANS 4:8 TLB

May 25

God's heart is the most sensitive and tender of all. No act goes unnoticed, no matter how insignificant or small.

RICHARD J. FOSTER

May 26

$\mathcal{A}$ cat is there when you call her—if she doesn't have anything better to do.

BILL ADLER

May 27

Happiness comes of the capacity
to feel deeply, to enjoy simply,
to think freely, to risk life, to be needed.

SAMUEL JAMESON

May 28

No matter how little money
and how few possessions, you own,
having a dog makes you rich.

LOUIS SABIN

May 29

$\mathcal{I}$ pray that you may enjoy good health
and that all may go well with you,
even as your soul is getting along well.

3 JOHN 1:2 NIV

May 30

Kittens are born with their eyes shut.
They open them in about six days,
take a look around, then close them
again for the better part of their lives.

STEPHEN BAKER

May 31

Nostalgia is the realization
that things weren't as unbearable
as they seemed at the time.

June 1

It is fatal to let any dog know that he is funny, for he immediately loses his head and starts hamming it up.

P. G. WODEHOUSE

June 2

Purring would seem to be, in her case,
an automatic safety-valve device
for dealing with happiness overflow.

MONICA EDWARDS

June 3

When we obey him, every path
he guides us on is fragrant with his
loving-kindness and his truth.

PSALM 25:10 TLB

June 4

Open your hearts to the love
God instills.... God loves you tenderly.
What He gives you is not to be kept
under lock and key, but to be shared.

MOTHER TERESA

June 5

Two things are aesthetically perfect in the world—the clock and the cat.

EMILE AUGUSTE CHARTIER

June 6

*L*ove is never lost. If not reciprocated,
it will flow back and soften
and purify the heart.

WASHINGTON IRVING

June 7

We become happier, much happier,
when we realize that life is an opportunity
rather than an obligation.

MARY AUGUSTINE

June 8

In everything you do, put God first,
and he will direct you and crown
your efforts with success.

PROVERBS 3:6 TLB

June 9

Outside of a dog, a book is man's best friend. Inside it's too dark to read.

GROUCHO MARX

June 10

When you're young and you fall off
a horse, you may break something.
When you're my age and you fall off,
you splatter.

Roy Rogers

June 11

I went to a restaurant that serves "breakfast at any time." So I ordered French Toast during the Renaissance.

STEVEN WRIGHT

June 12

*I*t is impossible to keep a straight face
in the presence of one or more kittens.

CYNTHIA E. VARNADO

June 13

The earth belongs to God! Everything in all the world is his! He is the one who pushed the oceans back to let dry land appear.

PSALM 24:1-2 TLB

June 14

*G*od has a wonderful plan for each
person.... He knew even before
He created this world what beauty
He would bring forth from our lives.

LOUIS B. WYLY

June 15

The wind rushing through the grass,
the thrush in the treetops,
and children tumbling in senseless
mirth stir in us a bright faith in life.

DONALD CULROSS PEATTIE

June 16

*M*y dog is worried about the economy
because Alpo is up to 99 cents a can.
That's almost $7.00 in dog money.

JOE WEINSTEIN

June 17

A cat isn't fussy—just so long as you remember he likes his milk in the shallow, rose-patterned saucer and his fish on the blue plate. From which he will take it, and eat it off the floor.

ARTHUR BRIDGES

June 18

As a father has compassion
on his children, so the Lord
has compassion on those who fear him.

PSALM 103:13 NIV

June 19

God wants His children to establish such
a close relationship with Him that
He becomes a natural partner in all
the experiences of life. That includes
those precious, happy times.

GLORIA GAITHER

June 20

*Y*ou will always be lucky
if you know how to make
friends with strange cats.

EARLY AMERICAN PROVERB

June 21

The clever cat eats cheese and breathes
down rat holes with baited breath.

W. C. FIELDS

June 22

Dad asks his daughter, "What are you doing with my toothbrush?" The daughter replies, "I'm brushing Spot's teeth. But don't worry Dad, I'll rinse it out when I'm done just like I always do."

June 23

*L*ove is very patient and kind,
  never jealous or envious,
  never boastful or proud.

I Corinthians 13:4 TLB

June 24

The smallest feline
is a masterpiece.

LEONARDO DA VINCI

June 25

A watchdog is a dog kept to guard your home, usually by sleeping where a burglar would awaken the household by falling over him.

June 26

Dear Lord, please help me to remember
to take the time to bestow the kisses today that
I want loved ones to remember tomorrow.

JENNIFER THOMAS

June 27

Encouragement is being a good listener,
being positive, letting others know you
accept them for who they are.
It is offering hope, caring about the feelings
of another, understanding.

GIGI GRAHAM TCHIVIDJIAN

June 28

Be delighted with the Lord. Then he will give you all your heart's desires. Commit everything you do to the Lord. Trust him to help you do it, and he will.

PSALM 37:4-5 TLB

June 29

Cats are intended to teach us that
not everything in nature has a purpose.

GARRISON KEILLOR

June 30

A cheerful friend is like a sunny day,
which sheds its brightness on all around.

JOHN LUBBOCK

A cheerful heart does good like medicine.

PROVERBS 17:22 TLB

July 1

No animal I know of can consistently be more of a friend and companion than a dog.

STANLEY LEINWOLL

July 2

If we love one another, God lives in us
and his love is made complete in us.

1 JOHN 4:12 NIV

July 3

When she walked...she stretched out long and thin like a little tiger, and held her head high to look over the grass as if she were treading the jungle.

SARAH ORNE JEWETT

July 4

I have been teaching patriotic songs to my children over the past few weeks. In a moment of inspiration, my 5-year-old daughter belted out, "O beautiful, our spaceship guys."

JANET SHELL

July 5

$\mathcal{I}$'m convinced more than ever that man finds liberation only when he binds himself to God and commits himself to his fellow man.

RONALD REAGAN

July 6

Oh, give thanks to the Lord, for he is so good! For his loving-kindness is forever.

PSALM 118:29 TLB

July 7

Snakes are not all bad. Some snakes are useful. One thing they are useful for is making belts.

A CHILD'S GARDEN OF MISINFORMATION

July 8

Never judge a dog's pedigree by the kind of books he does not chew.

July 9

*G*od's will is doing those things
we know to be right for each day
and doing them the best we possibly can.

GLORIA GAITHER

July 10

May the Lord continually bless you with
heaven's blessings as well as with human joys.

PSALM 128:5 TLB

July 11

Most cats, when they are out want to be in, and vice versa, and often simultaneously.

Louis J. Camuti

July 12

I love cats because they are so beautiful
aesthetically. They are like sculpture
walking around the house.

WANDA TOSCANINI HOROWITZ

July 13

$\mathcal{A}$ word of encouragement to those we meet, a cheerful smile in the supermarket, a card or letter to a friend, a readiness to witness when opportunity is given— all are practical ways in which we may let His light shine through us.

ELIZABETH B. JONES

July 14

Old dogs, like old shoes, are comfortable.
They might be a bit out of shape and a little
worn around the edges, but they fit well.

BONNIE WILCOX

July 15

The only thing that counts is faith
expressing itself through love.

GALATIANS 5:6 NIV

July 16

Generally, by the time you are Real, most of your hair has been loved off, and your eyes drop out and you get loose in the joints and very shabby. But these things don't matter at all, because once you are Real you can't be ugly, except to people who don't understand.

MARGERY WILLIAMS

July 17

*Y*our best friend is the person who brings
out of you the best that is within you.

HENRY FORD

July 18

An intellectual snob is someone who
can listen to the William Tell Overture
and not think of The Lone Ranger.

DAN RATHER

July 19

I once decided not to date a guy because he wasn't excited to meet my dog. I mean, this was like not wanting to meet my mother.

BONNIE SCHACTER

July 20

A mirror reflects a man's face,
but what he is really like is shown
by the kind of friends he chooses.

PROVERBS 27:19 TLB

July 21

Cats were put into the world
to disprove the dogma that all things
were created to serve man.

PAUL GRAY

July 22

A leading authority is anyone who has guessed right more than once.

July 23

A door is what a dog is perpetually
on the wrong side of.

OGDEN NASH

I spilled spot remover on my dog.
He's gone now.

STEVEN WRIGHT

July 24

For a man to truly understand rejection,
he must first be ignored by a cat.

July 25

*P*leasant words are a honeycomb, sweet to the soul and healing to the bones.

PROVERBS 16:24 NIV

July 26

Whoever said you can't buy happiness
forgot about little puppies.

GENE HILL

July 27

When we recall the past, we usually find that it is the simplest things—not the great occasions—that in retrospect give off the greatest glow of happiness.

BOB HOPE

July 28

A friend is one who believes in
you before you believe in yourself.

July 29

The reason a dog has so many friends is that he wags his tail instead of his tongue.

July 30

May you be given more and more
of God's kindness, peace, and love.

JUDE 1:2 TLB

July 31

If your dog is fat, you aren't
getting enough exercise.

Never trust a dog to watch your food.

PATRICK, AGE 10

August 1

Thank goodness for August—the time to lie back and wallow in the knowledge that there is absolutely no occasion to rise to.

BARBARA JOHNSON

August 2

The real measure of a day's heat
is the length of a sleeping cat.

August 3

A dog is a man's best friend and when
he licks you it is not from beating you up,
it is from getting you wet.

A CHILD'S GARDEN OF MISINFORMATION

August 4

Whoever pursues righteousness and
kindness will find life and honor.

PROVERBS 21:21 NRSV

August 5

Moments spent listening, talking, playing, and sharing together may be the most important times of all.

GLORIA GAITHER

August 6

There are two means of refuge from the misery of life—music and cats.

ALBERT SCHWIETZER

August 7

There has never been a cat who couldn't calm
me down by walking slowly past my chair.

ROD McKUEN

August 8

Life is not intended to be simply a round
of work, no matter how interesting and
important that work may be. A moment's
pause to watch the glory of a sunrise or
a sunset is soul satisfying, while a bird's song
will set the steps to music all day long.

LAURA INGALLS WILDER

August 9

These three remain: faith, hope and love.
But the greatest of these is love.
Follow the way of love.

1 Corinthians 13:13-14:1 niv

August 10

One is never sure, watching two cats washing each other, whether it's affection, the taste, or a trial run for the jugular.

HELEN THOMSON

August 11

Church blooper: While Pastor is
on vacation, massages can be given
to church secretary.

August 12

If you think dogs can't count, try putting three dog biscuits in your pocket and then giving Fido only two of them.

PHIL PASTORET

August 13

I'm living so far beyond my income that we may almost be said to be living apart.

August 14

A generous man will prosper; he who
refreshes others will himself be refreshed.

PROVERBS 11:25 NIV

August 15

Always be in a state of expectancy,
and see that you leave room for God
to come in as He likes.

OSWALD CHAMBERS

August 16

Cats have intercepted my footsteps
at the ankle for so long that my gait, both
at home and on tour, has been compared
to that of a man wading through low surf.

ROY BLOUNT JR.

August 17

The abundant life that Jesus talked
about begins with the unfathomable
Good News put simply:
My dear child, I love you anyway.

ALICE CHAPIN

August 18

*L*obsters only wear their backbones
on their outsides, like somebody only
thought of it at the last minute.

A CHILDREN'S GARDEN OF MISINFORMATION.

August 19

O Lord, you have examined my heart
and you know everything about me.
You know when I sit or stand. When far
away you know my every thought.... You both
precede and follow me, and place your
hand of blessing on my head.

PSALM 139:1-2,5 TLB

August 20

God is never in a hurry but spends years
with those He expects to greatly use.
He never thinks the days of preparation
too long or too dull.

L. B. COWMAN

August 21

My wife, Shirley, and I have felt
for years that laughter was one of the keys
to the success of our family and relationship.
We simply have fun being together.

JAMES DOBSON

August 22

Animals are reliable, many full of love,
true in their affections, predictable
in their actions, grateful and loyal.
Difficult standards for people to live up to.

ALFRED A. MONTAPERT

August 23

You are in the Beloved...therefore
infinitely dear to the Father,
unspeakably precious to Him.
You are never, not for one second, alone.

NORMAN DOWTY

August 24

May the Lord make your love increase
and overflow for each other.

1 Thessalonians 3:12 niv

August 25

God looks at the heart. Let others look at the outward appearances—if that's what they want to do. They won't be looking at the true measure of our worth.

August 26

*I*f you want a kitten,
start out by asking for a horse.

NAOMI, 15

*D*iplomacy—the art of letting
someone have your way.

August 27

Among animals, cats are
the top-hatted, frock-coated statesmen
going about their affairs at their own pace.

ROBERT STEARNS

August 28

The other day I saw two dogs walk over to a parking meter. One of them says to the other, "How do you like that? Pay toilets!"

DAVE STARR

August 29

Now glory be to God who by his mighty power at work within us is able to do far more than we would ever dare to ask or even dream of—infinitely beyond our highest prayers, desires, thoughts or hopes.

Ephesians 3:20 tlb

August 30

My goal in life is to be as good
of a person my dog already thinks I am.

August 31

To be truly happy is a question of how
we begin and not of how we end,
of what we want and not of what we have.

ROBERT LOUIS STEVENSON

September 1

My daughter was getting poor grades in school. She seemed very concerned about her teacher. One day she tapped her teacher on the shoulder and said, "I don't want to scare you, but my daddy says if I don't get better grades somebody is going to get a spanking!"

September 2

I think animal testing is a terrible idea; they get all nervous and give the wrong answers

JOSEPH BLOSEPHINA

September 3

Be glad for all God is planning for you.
Be patient in trouble, and prayerful always.

ROMANS 12:12 TLB

September 4

We may not all reach God's ideal for us, but with His help we may move in that direction day by day as we relate every detail of our lives to Him.

CAROL GISH

September 5

Children and dogs are as necessary
to the welfare of the country
as Wall Street and the railroads.

HARRY S. TRUMAN

September 6

I always try to go the extra mile at work, but my boss always finds me and brings me back.

September 7

If you have made mistakes...there is always another chance for you.... You may have a fresh start any moment you choose, for this thing we call "failure" is not the falling down, but the staying down.

MARY PICKFORD

September 8

You have welcomed me as your guest;
blessings overflow! Your goodness
and unfailing kindness shall
be with me all of my life.

Psalm 23:5-6 TLB

September 9

A good dog…walks beside you
on crisp autumn days when frost is on the
fields and winter's drawing near, his head
is within your hand in his old way.

MARY CAROLYN DAVIES

September 10

"Carpe Diem" does not mean
"fish of the day".

Now is the time.

HEBREWS 3:15 TLB

September 11

Friends rush in where reason fears to tread.

Perfect love drives out fear.

1 JOHN 4:18 NIV

September 12

$\mathcal{E}$very time Jesus sees that there
is a possibility of giving us more than
we know how to ask, He does so.

OLE HALLESBY

September 13

The Lord is good to all, and his
compassion is over all that he has made.

PSALM 145:9 NRSV

September 14

*N*ever hold a dust buster
and a cat at the same time.

KYOYA, 9

September 15

Friends...lift our spirits, keep us honest,
stick with us when times are tough,
and make mundane tasks enjoyable.
No wonder we want to make friends.

EM GRIFFIN

September 16

Did you know that dolphins are
so intelligent that within only a few weeks
of captivity, they can train Americans
to stand at the very edge of the pool
and throw them fish.

September 17

There's just something about dogs
that makes you feel good.
You come home, they're thrilled
to see you. They're good for the ego.

JANET SCHNELLMAN

September 18

Say only what is good and helpful
to those you are talking to,
and what will give them a blessing.

EPHESIANS 4:29 TLB

September 19

Puppies are nature's remedy for feeling unloved...plus numerous other aliments of life.

RICHARD ALLAN PALM

September 20

Everyone has a unique role to fill
in the world and is important in some respect.
Everyone, including and perhaps
especially you, is indispensable.

NATHANIEL HAWTHORNE

September 21

Did you ever see an unhappy horse?
Did you ever see a bird that has the blues?
One reason why birds and horses are not
unhappy is because they are not trying
to impress other birds and horses.

DALE CARNEGIE

September 22

Our mouths were filled with laughter,
our tongues with songs of joy. Then it was
said among the nations, "The Lord has done
great things for them." The Lord has done
great things for us, and we are filled with joy.

PSALM 126:2-3 NIV

September 23

I read recipes the same way I read science fiction. I get to the end and think, "Well, that's not going to happen."

September 24

We've got a cat called Ben Hur.
We called it Ben till it had kittens.

SALLY POPLIN

September 25

If God, like a father, denies us what
we want now, it is in order to give us some
far better thing later on. The will of God,
we can rest assured, is invariably a better thing.

ELISABETH ELLIOT

September 26

Pumas are mountain lions.
Little ones are called pumice.

A CHILD'S GARDEN OF MISINFORMATION

September 27

$\mathcal{B}$e completely humble and gentle;
be patient, bearing with one another in love.

EPHESIANS 4:2 NIV

September 28

We are so preciously loved by God that we cannot even comprehend it. No created being can ever know how much and how sweetly and tenderly God loves them.

JULIAN OF NORWICH

September 29

$\mathcal{I}$ believe that God is in me as the sun
is in the color and fragrance of a flower.

<small>HELEN KELLER</small>

September 30

$\mathcal{E}$ven the tiniest poodle is lionhearted,
ready to do anything to defend home,
master, and mistress.

LOUIS SABIN

October 1

You give [us] drink from the river
of your delights. For with you
is the fountain of life;
in your light we see light.

PSALM 36:8-9 NRSV

October 2

God made the cat in order
that human kind might have
the pleasure of caressing the tiger.

FERNAND MERY

October 3

A dog is one of the remaining reasons
why some people can be persuaded
to go for a walk.

O. A. BATTISTA

October 4

$\mathcal{U}$nlike us, cats never outgrow their delight in cat capacities, nor do they settle finally for limitations. Cats, I think, live out their lives fulfilling their expectations.

IRVING TOWNSEND

October 5

To understand and to be understood
makes our happiness on earth.

GERMAN PROVERB

October 6

The Lord longs to be gracious to you;
he rises to show you compassion....
Blessed are all who wait for him.

ISAIAH 30:18 NIV

October 7

Some of the world's greatest feats were accomplished by people not smart enough to know they were impossible.

DOUG LARSON

October 8

Dogs come when they're called; cats take
a message and get back to you later.

MARY BLY

October 9

Often God has to shut a door in our face,
so that He can subsequently open the door
through which He wants us to go.

CATHERINE MARSHALL

October 10

I went to a bookstore
and asked the saleswoman,
"Where's the self-help section?"
She said if she told me,
it would defeat the purpose.

STEVEN WRIGHT

October 11

*Y*our heavenly Father knows your needs.
He will always give you all you
need from day to day.

LUKE 12:30-31 TLB

October 12

There is no snooze button
on a cat who wants breakfast.

October 13

When I look back at where I've been,
I see that what I am becoming is a whole lot
further down the road from where I was.

GLORIA GAITHER

October 14

God's promises are like the stars; the darker
the night the brighter they shine.

DAVID NICHOLAS

October 15

Anyone who doesn't know what soap tastes like never washed a dog.

FRANKLIN P. JONES

October 16

$\mathcal{M}$ay the Lord of peace himself give you peace at all times and in every way.

2 Thessalonians 3:16 niv

October 17

A recent census taken among cats shows that approximately one hundred percent are neurotic. That estimate is probably low.

STEPHEN BAKER

October 18

If you believe in a God who controls
the big things, you have to believe in a God
who controls the little things. It is we,
of course, to whom things look "little" or "big."

ELISABETH ELLIOT

October 19

*L*ift up your eyes. Your heavenly Father waits
to bless you—in inconceivable ways to make
your life what you never dreamed it could be.

ANNE ORTLUND

October 20

They say the test of literary power is whether
a man can write an inscription.
I say, "Can he name a kitten?"

SAMUEL BUTLER

October 21

Be beautiful inside, in your hearts, with the lasting charm of a gentle and quiet spirit which is precious to God.

I Peter 3:4 TLB

October 22

Encouragement is awesome.
It has the capacity...to actually
change the course of another
human being's day, week, or life.

CHARLES SWINDOLL

October 23

When someone is having a bad day,
be silent, sit close by, and nuzzle them gently.

October 24

I'd be happy to have my biography
be the stories of my dogs. To me,
to live without dogs would mean
accepting a form of blindness.

THOMAS MCGUANE

October 25

Use what talents you possess:
the woods would be very silent if no birds
sang there except those that sang best.

HENRY VAN DYKE

October 26

God has given each of you some special abilities; be sure to use them to help each other, passing on to others God's many kinds of blessings.

I PETER 4:10 TLB

October 27

*L*ife is God's gift to you.
The way you live your life is your
gift to God. Make it a fantastic one.

LEO BUSCAGLIA

October 28

I love a dog. He does nothing
for political reasons.

WILL ROGERS

*D*umb dog. I bought a dog whistle.
He won't use it.

October 29

Laughter is like changing a baby's diaper—it doesn't permanently solve any problems, but it makes things more acceptable for a while.

October 30

The real secret of happiness is not what you give or what you receive; it's what you share.

October 31

Come, let us sing for joy to the Lord....
Let us come before him with thanksgiving.

PSALM 95:1-2 NIV

November 1

*E*ver consider what they must think of us?
I mean, here we come back from a grocery
store with the most amazing haul—chicken,
pork, half a cow. They must think we're
the greatest hunters on earth!

ANNE TYLER

November 2

Nothing enters your life accidentally—
remember that. Behind our every
experience is our loving, sovereign God.

CHARLES SWINDOLL

November 3

The wisdom that comes from heaven
is first of all pure; then peace-loving,
considerate, submissive, full of mercy
and good fruit, impartial and sincere.

JAMES 3:17 NIV

November 4

The one thing I do not want to be called
is First Lady. It sounds like a saddle horse.

JACQUELINE KENNEDY

November 5

Some people say man is the most dangerous animal on the planet. Obviously those people have never met an angry cat.

LILLIAN JOHNSON

November 6

The really happy person is one who can enjoy the scenery on a detour.

November 7

In whatever [God] does in the course
of our lives, He gives us, through
the experience, some power to help others.

ELISABETH ELLIOT

November 8

My children, we should love people
not only with words and talk,
but by our actions and true caring.

1 JOHN 3:18 NCV

November 9

A horse's behavior will
be in direct proportion to the number
of people watching you ride him.

COOKY MCLUNG

November 10

Celebration is more than a happy feeling. Celebration is an experience. It is liking others, accepting others, laughing with others.

DOUGLAS STUVA

November 11

When one door closes, another door always opens—but those long hallways are a real drag.

PATTY WOOTEN

November 12

Prowling his own quiet backyard
or asleep by the fire, he is still only
a whisker away from the wilds.

JEAN BURDEN

November 13

For the Spirit of God has made me,
and the breath of the Almighty gives me life.

JOB 33:4 TLB

November 14

The misery of keeping a dog is his
dying so soon. But, to be sure,
if he lived for fifty years and then died,
what would become of me?

SIR WALTER SCOTT

November 15

Joyfulness keeps the heart and face young.
A good laugh makes us better friends with
ourselves and everybody around us.

ORISON SWETT MARDEN

November 16

I would maintain that thanks are
the highest form of thought, and that
gratitude is happiness doubled by wonder.

G. K. CHESTERTON

November 17

$\mathscr{I}$ have learned more from my dog than
from all the great books I have read.
The wisdom of my dog is the product
of his inability to conceal his wants.
When he yearns to be loved…he puts
his head on my lap, wags his tail and looks
up at me with kind eyes, waiting to be petted.

GERRY SPENCE

November 18

Give generously...because of this the Lord your God will bless you in all your work and in everything you put your hand to.

DEUTERONOMY 15:10 NIV

November 19

Whether we are poets or parents
or teachers or artists or gardeners,
we must start where we are and use what
we have. In the process of creation
and relationship, what seems mundane
and trivial may show itself to be holy,
precious, part of a pattern.

LUCI SHAW

November 20

Cats are absolute individuals,
with their own ideas about everything,
including the people they own.

JOHN DINGMAN

November 21

A kitten is so flexible that she
is almost double; the hind parts are equivalent
to another kitten with which the forepart
plays. She does not discover that her tail
belongs to her until you tread on it.

HENRY DAVID THOREAU

November 22

To be grateful is to recognize the love
of God in everything He has given
us—and He has given us everything.

THOMAS MERTON

November 23

For the Lord is always good. He is always loving and kind, and his faithfulness goes on and on to each succeeding generation.

PSALM 100:5 TLB

November 24

Old Yeller was bought for 3 dollars from
a shelter; his real name was Spike.
Disney's "Shaggy Dog" was bought
for 2 dollars at a pound.

WORLD FEATURES SYNDICATE

November 25

He from whom all blessings flow must not be forgotten. A call for a national thanksgiving is being prepared.

ABRAHAM LINCOLN

November 26

A good day: When the wheels of your shopping cart all go in the same direction.

November 27

A morning kiss, a discreet touch
of his nose landing somewhere on the middle
of my face. Because his long white whiskers
tickled, I begin each day laughing.

JANET F. FAURE

November 28

*G*ive generously, for your gifts
will return to you later.

ECCLESIASTES 11:1 TLB

November 29

Yesterday I was a dog.
Today I'm a dog.
Tomorrow I'll probably still be a dog.
Sigh! There's so little hope for advancement.

CHARLES SCHULZ

November 30

Cat people are different,
to the extent that they generally
are not conformists. How could
they be, with a cat running their lives?

LOUIS J. CAMUTI

December 1

You pay God a compliment
by asking great things of Him.

TERESA OF AVILA

December 2

The mark of a true friend—someone who lets you sit on the heater vent first.

December 3

This is what I have asked of God for you:
that you will be encouraged and knit
together by strong ties of love.

COLOSSIANS 2:2 TLB

December 4

Laughing at ourselves as well as with each other gives a surprising sense of togetherness.

HAZEL C. LEE

December 5

$\mathcal{E}$very day we live is a priceless gift of God,
loaded with possibilities to learn something
new, to gain fresh insights.

DALE EVANS ROGERS

December 6

I guess a cat is sort of like a poem.
A cat is relatively short. A cat is only subtly
demonstrative. To be sure, you can curl
up with a good cat, but that doesn't
mean you understand the cat.

ROY BLOUNT JR.

December 7

*Y*ou chart the path ahead of me,
and tell me where to stop and rest.
Every moment, you know where I am....
You both precede and follow me, and place
your hand of blessing on my head.

PSALM 139:3,5 TLB

December 8

An inexhaustible good nature is one
of the most precious gifts of heaven,
spreading itself like oil over the troubled
sea of thought, and keeping the mind smooth
and equable in the roughest weather.

WASHINGTON IRVING

December 9

Money can't buy success—but somehow
it is more comfortable to cry
in a Porshe than a Yugo.

December 10

It doesn't take great wisdom to energize
a person, but it does take sixty seconds.
That's the amount of time it takes to walk
over and gently hold someone we love.

GARY SMALLEY AND JOHN TRENT

December 11

A dog will often steal a bone,
But conscience lets him not alone,
And by his tail his guilt is known.
But cats consider theft a game,
And howsoever you may blame,
Refuse the slightest sign of shame.

December 12

*In your presence there is fullness of joy;
at your right hand are pleasures forevermore.*

PSALM 16:11 NRSV

December 13

To do great and important tasks,
two things are necessary:
a plan and not quite enough time.

December 14

$\mathcal{M}$an loves the dog because the dog
is fool enough to trust man.
On the other hand, the cat obeys Scriptures:
"Put not thy trust in things."

MELVIN B. TOLSON

December 15

It's good to have money and the things
that money can buy, but it's good, too,
to check up once in a while and make sure
you haven't lost the things that money can't
buy.

GEORGE HORACE LORIMER

December 16

I bought a dog the other day...I named him
Stay. It's fun to call him..."Come here, Stay!
Come here, Stay!" He went insane.
Now he just ignores me and keeps typing.

STEVEN WRIGHT

December 17

May your roots go down deep into the soil
of God's marvelous love; and may you be able
to feel and understand...how long, how wide,
how deep, and how high his love really is.

EPHESIANS 3:17,18 TLB

December 18

God's gifts make us truly wealthy.
His loving supply never
shall leave us wanting.

<small>BECKY LAIRD</small>

December 19

Christmas is a time of the heart,
not just a date.
Its meaning transcends time.

December 20

I know that dogs are pack animals,
but it is difficult to imagine a pack
of standard poodles...and if there was
such a thing as a pack of standard poodles,
where would they rove to? Bloomingdale's?

Yvonne Clifford

December 21

The most precious gift that one person can bestow upon another is gentle encouragement.

W. PHILLIP KELLER

December 22

It is good to be children sometimes,
and never better than at Christmas,
when its mighty Founder was a child Himself.

CHARLES DICKENS

December 23

When you have laboriously
accomplished your daily task,
go to sleep in peace. God is awake.

VICTOR HUGO

December 24

The coming of Jesus at Bethlehem brought joy to the world and to every human heart. May His coming this Christmas bring to each one of us that peace and joy that He desires to give.

MOTHER TERESA

December 25

*L*isten! The virgin shall conceive a child!
She shall give birth to a Son,
and he shall be called "Emmanuel"
(meaning "God is with us").

MATTHEW 1:23 TLB

December 26

The cat could very well be man's best friend
but would never stoop to admitting it.

DOUG LARSON

December 27

You should be like one big happy
family...loving one another
with tender hearts and humble minds.

I Peter 3:8 TLB

December 28

Butterflies are at first long worms.
But then they start living right.

A CHILD'S GARDEN OF MISINFORMATION

December 29

Old age means realizing you will never own all the dogs you wanted to.

JOE GORES

December 30

$\mathcal{I}$ am confident that the Almighty has His plans, and will work them out; and, whether we see it or not, they will be the best for us.

ABRAHAM LINCOLN

December 31

Thank the Lord, it is His love that arranges
our tomorrows—and we may be certain
that whatever tomorrow brings,
His love sent it our way.

CHARLES SWINDOLL